Contents

Introduction 4

Templates and
    brooch backs 6

Swaddling Sister 8

Artemis Ascendent 10

Daffy-Down-Dilly 12

Bonnie Wee Rosie 14

Babouska 16

Rustic Peg 18

Luna Luna 20

The Queen of Fools 22

Ikon 24

Jokergirl 26

Mary, Mary,
    By-the-Sea 28

Nefertiti 30

Miss Milly-Pede 32

Cherokee 34

Oh, Pearl! 36

Miss Checkmate 38

Wild Wanda 40

Tart Deco 42

San Bohemia 44

Dreamer 46

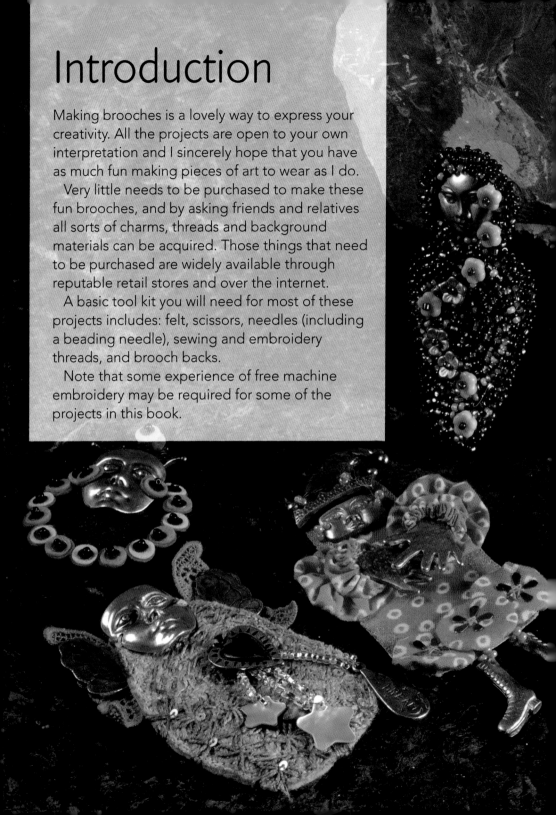

Introduction

Making brooches is a lovely way to express your creativity. All the projects are open to your own interpretation and I sincerely hope that you have as much fun making pieces of art to wear as I do.

Very little needs to be purchased to make these fun brooches, and by asking friends and relatives all sorts of charms, threads and background materials can be acquired. Those things that need to be purchased are widely available through reputable retail stores and over the internet.

A basic tool kit you will need for most of these projects includes: felt, scissors, needles (including a beading needle), sewing and embroidery threads, and brooch backs.

Note that some experience of free machine embroidery may be required for some of the projects in this book.

Templates and brooch backs

Each of the projects in this book uses one of the four templates shown here. Each of these templates has been reproduced at full size, ready to be used.

Finishing off the brooch

Apart from the instructions in the project, you may choose to hide any untidy thread ends on the back of the brooch by cutting out an extra medium weight template to match the body shape and colour. Place it on the back of the brooch, then depending on the design, either oversew the edges, or attach the back to the front with invisible or matching thread.

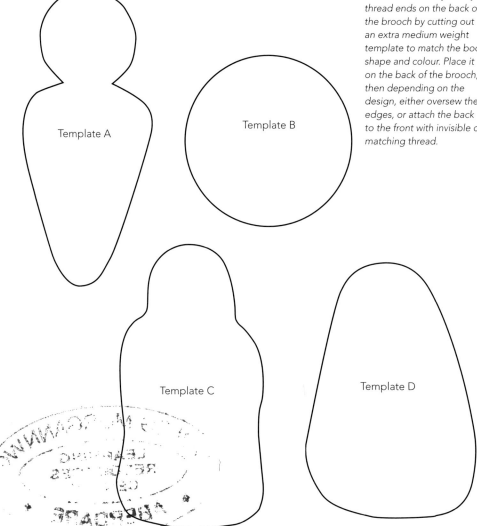

Template A

Template B

Template C

Template D

Once you have completed each Wild Woman, you will need to afix a brooch back to the finished piece. There are numerous different types, from brass backs that can be stitched on, to simple adhesive backs as shown above.

The positioning of the brooch back is very important: make sure you attach it within the top third of the piece, so that the piece hangs well when being worn. If you place the back too low down, the top can curl over.

Swaddling Sister

Materials:

Lilac, blue, gold and
   purple seed beads

Eight flower-shaped
   feature beads

One face charm

Template A cut out
   of non-woven white
   heavy interlining

Template A cut out of non-
   woven black medium
   weight interlining

Tools:

Basic tool kit

Blue felt-tipped pen

Instructions:

1 Using the blue felt-tipped pen, colour one side of the heavy interlining template. This makes any spaces between the beads less obvious.

2 Sew on the face charm with the needle and thread.

3 Outline the charm with a mix of all of the seed beads, then continue to fill in the rest of the body with beads. Stitch in groups of three beads as this allows gentle curves to be made. Leave a 2mm (¹⁄₁₆in) gap around the edge of the template.

4 Stitch feature beads on in a trailing line, using a seed bead on each to anchor them in place (see detail opposite).

5 Place the medium weight interlining on the back. Using groups of three to five seed beads, oversew the two edges until a rope-like effect is created all around the template.

6 Attach a brooch back to complete the piece.

Ruby!

Using a variety of flower-shaped feature beads and warmer colours changes the feel of the brooch dramatically.

Artemis Ascendent

Materials:

White cotton, approximately 15cm (6in) square

Black solvent-based permanent ink pad

A 15cm (6in) piece of black non-woven medium weight interlining

A 15cm (6in) piece of non-woven white heavy weight interlining

Pink and blue fabric paints

Small amount of wadding

Magenta (18009F) face stamp

Permanent black marker pen

Nine silver sequins

Nine seed beads

Tools:

Basic tool kit

Paintbrush

Pencil

Sewing machine

Instructions:

1 Use the face stamp to print a face on to the cotton with the permanent ink pad and allow to dry.

2 Draw template B around the printed motif with the pencil, then place the cotton on to the medium weight interlining.

3 Using the sewing machine, stitch around the outline of the face motif and the outer circle, then cut away the excess fabric.

4 Mark the triangles with the permanent black marker pen to plan out a pattern of triangles round the outer ring, then use the fabric paints to colour them. Make sure you paint over the outer stitch line as this will prevent fraying. Allow to dry.

5 Cut small slits in the interlining from the back and stuff the face and outer halo with wadding to give a gentle raised effect. Stitch the background closed.

6 Cut a piece of non-woven heavy interlining to cover the back, then use simple hand stitches and a few sequins and beads (see detail opposite) to secure the interlining and decorate the halo.

7 Stitch or glue a brooch back in position on the back to complete the brooch.

Diana Resplendent

An irregular border on the halo gives a pleasing varied effect to the finished piece and is very simple to do.

Daffy-Down-Dilly

Materials:

Artgirlz Heart and Face rubber stamps

Black and red solvent-based permanent ink pads

Template A cut from cotton

Template A cut from non-woven black
heavy interlining

Template A cut from non-woven white medium
weight interlining

A selection of orange and green seed beads

Eleven gold flower sequins

Heart and star feature beads

Tools:

Basic tool kit

Sewing machine

Instructions:

1 Print the face and heart stamps on to the cotton template using black and red ink pads respectively.

2 Attach the printed cotton template to the medium interlining template by carefully stitching around the outline of the face and heart with orange cotton thread.

3 Use free machine embroidery to fill the remaining space.

4 Attach the flower sequins around the face, securing each with a seed bead (see detail opposite), then attach beads all around the heart and face.

5 To create the fringe effect, take a needle up through the interlining and thread three orange seed beads, then a heart feature bead, then a single green seed bead on to the needle.

6 Miss the green bead out and pass the needle back through the feature bead and orange beads above. Take the needle back down through the interlining and secure to create the first part of the fringe.

7 Continue working along the fringe at the bottom and below the central heart shape, varying the number of seed beads and feature beads on each part as shown opposite.

8 Stitch the heavy interlining template on to the back, then glue or stitch a brooch back on to the piece to finish.

Polly Potter
Sometimes subtle changes in colour can make a difference, as shown in this variation.

Bonnie Wee Rosie

Materials:

Clearsnap 'Cosmic Faces' style stone

Orange, red, gold and silver acrylic paint

Heart feature charm

7.5cm (3in) circle of white cotton

A selection of seed beads

Template B, cut from non-woven white medium weight interlining

Tools:

Basic tool kit

Paintbrush

Glue

Instructions:

1 Use the orange, red and gold paints to colour the style stone.

2 Using orange, red and silver paint, colour the 7.5cm (3in) circle of cotton and allow to dry.

3 Gather the circle inwards to form the outer frill using tiny running stitches. Manipulate until the gathered circle is approximately 5cm (2in) across.

4 Stitch the style stone on top of the gathers. If the style stone does not cover the stitching tighten the gathering until it does. If the style stone is loose then a small amount of glue may be put on the back to provide a more secure attachment to the cotton.

5 Embellish the cotton circle by sewing on seed beads in groups of three (see detail) with orange thread, then attach the heart feature charm on the lower edge with a string of seed beads as shown.

6 Sew single seed beads round the edge of the circle.

7 Finish by sewing on the medium weight interlining piece and brooch back on to the back of the piece.

Evening Star

More muted colours of paint were used here, emphasising the bright colours of the seed beads. The star charm echoes the star-shaped style stone.

Babouska

Materials:

Template C cut from non-woven black medium weight interlining

Template C cut from pink craft felt

Pink 7mm (¼in) sheer ribbon

Bronze sequins and red seed beads.

Two arm charms, two leg charms

Artgirlz 'Mini Face' charm

Tools:

Basic tool kit

Instructions:

1 Cut at least thirty lengths of ribbon, each approximately 6cm (2¼in).

2 Using the needle and pink thread, sew tiny running stitches along one edge of a length of ribbon, then gather it into a rosette.

3 Secure the rosette with a small stitch and lay to one side. Repeat on the other ribbons until you have enough rosettes to cover the felt template.

4 Sew the face charm into position on to the felt and then fasten each rosette in place by stitching on a sequin with a seed bead in the centre (see detail).

5 Use a needle and thread to attach the arms and legs into position on the body.

6 When complete, stitch or glue the brooch back to the medium weight interlining and glue or stitch the brooch to the back of the body to finish.

Harlequin

Try using many different ribbons for a multicoloured effect. If you wish, a garter can be made from a length of the ribbon and attached around a leg.

17

Rustic Peg

Materials:

Small oval style stone

Artgirlz charms: two 'Bent Arm' and two 'Striped Boot'

Artgirlz stamps: 'Dream It' face and 'Be Bold' dress

Black solvent-based permanent ink pad

5cm (2in) square piece of lightweight silk

Small amount of lace

Yellow and blue solvent-based peel-off marker pens

Template D cut from non-woven white heavy interlining

Bronze acrylic paint

Blue and yellow fabric paints

Tools:

Basic tool kit

Paintbrush

Instructions:

1 Using the black ink pad, stamp the face on to the oval style stone, then use the dress stamp three times to form a fan shape on the lightweight silk.

2 Cut out the dress shape and paint in the stamped flowers and background using the blue and yellow fabric paints.

3 Once the fabric paints have dried, use the bronze acrylic paint to paint the edge of the style stone and outline the dress. The paint forms a seal and prevents the fabric from fraying.

4 While you wait for this to dry, sew a frill of lace on to the bottom edge of the heavy interlining template.

5 Gather the dress at the neck before stitching down and sewing the fabric into position to form gentle pleats. Sew the dress into place on the heavy interlining template.

6 Stitch lace around the edge of the neck line to form a ruff.

7 Colour the legs and arms with the yellow and blue peel-off marker pens.

8 Carefully position the arm charms underneath the ruff, then sew them on.

9 Stitch the face into position, then create the hair by stitching an area of French knots (see detail opposite).

10 Stitch the leg charms into position and finish by gluing or stitching a brooch back to the piece.

Goldilocks

This variation has blonde hair made with pale creamy-yellow French knots.

Luna Luna

Materials:

Clearsnap 'Cosmic Faces'
   style stone

Black and white acrylic paint

Black, white and gold
   seed beads

Template B cut from non-woven
   black heavy interlining

Template B cut from non-woven
   black medium weight interlining

Tools:

Basic tool kit

Paintbrush

Instructions:

1 Paint the style stone face with shades of grey made up with a mix of black and white acrylic paints. Allow to dry.

2 Sew it to the middle of the heavy interlining template.

3 For the first row, stitch groups of seven black and white beads to the interlining in loops all around the face.

4 For the second row, stitch groups of eleven black and white beads in loops all around the first row.

5 For the third row, stitch groups of thirteen black, white and gold beads in loops all around the second row.

6 To finish the edge, attach the medium weight interlining to the heavy interlining with groups of three gold beads stitched so that they form a rope-like effect (see detail opposite) around the edge.

7 Complete the piece by attaching a brooch back.

Morningstar
Use fifteen beads on the loops of the third row for a star-like effect.

The Queen of Fools

Materials:

Template C cut from patterned green cotton

Template C cut from non-woven white heavy interlining

Five copies of template B cut from patterned green cotton

Two 5.5cm (2¼in) circles of patterned green cotton

Three flower sequins

Ten small beads

Green, blue and gold peel-off marker pens

Gold fabric paint

Artgirlz charms: two 'Cartoon Hand', two 'Laced Boot', one 'Mini Face' and one 'Elf Hat'

Tools:

Basic tool kit

Paintbrush

Medium weight fusable web

Instructions:

1 Attach the patterned green cotton template C to the heavy interlining using the fusable web. Be sure to follow the manufacturer's instructions.

2 Paint around the edge with gold fabric paint to prevent fraying.

3 Colour the face, hat, hand and leg charms with the peel-off marker pens to co-ordinate with the green cotton.

4 Make all the fabric circles into puffs by stitching around the edge and gathering them. The cuffs should be folded over and then stitched and gathered to form a neat presentation.

5 Sew the larger puffs to the heavy interlining as shoulders, then sew a smaller puff in the centre of each with the cuffs showing. Sew the hand charms in the centre of the cuffs (see detail opposite).

6 Sew the remaining puffs to the bottom edge of the body, making sure the cuffs are face-down and hidden. Embellish each one with decorative sequins.

7 Sew the legs on, making sure the tops are hidden by the puffs at the bottom.

8 Use the needle and thread to attach the hat and face charms, adding small beads to embellish and add interest to them.

9 Complete by gluing or stitching a brooch back to the piece.

Joker

This cheeky character would make a great gift for the family comedian!
The legs are attached with a ring of seed beads, which lets them dangle.

Ikon

Materials:

Sixteen gold beads

Pink, purple, gold, red and
turquoise acrylic paint

Two copies of template A
cut from non-woven
white heavy interlining

Tools:

Basic tool kit

Sizzex hand die-cut
system (heart)

Paintbrush

Glue

Instructions:

1 Use the red and gold paints to decorate one side of the first template – gold at the head and red for the body. Allow to dry.

2 Paint the other template with the pink, purple, turquoise and gold paints and allow to dry.

3 Use the die-cutter to cut a heart shape out of the second painted template. Keep the section removed and paint the back and edges in the same colours.

4 Use sharp scissors to cut out a circle from the head of the second template.

5 Glue the two pieces together so that the red and gold parts of the first template show through the holes in the second. When the glue is dry, paint gold around the edges. Allow to dry.

6 Stitch ten gold beads on to the piece around the head (see detail opposite) and attach the punched-out heart with the remaining beads so that it dangles from the bottom of the body.

7 Attach an adhesive brooch back to the piece.

Devotion

Most small die-cut shapes will work with this simple and elegant brooch. Here, a small star is used as an eye-catching design

Jokergirl

Materials:

Artgirlz charms: one 'Girl Face' and one 'Create Crown'

Green and brown peel-off marker pens

Sixteen small gold sequins

Sixteen black seed beads

Template B cut from non-woven black medium weight interlining

Green, orange and yellow pieces of non-woven medium weight interlining

Tools:

Basic tool kit

Small circle punch

Glue

Instructions:

1 Position the head charm slightly above the top edge of the first interlining template and sew it on.

2 Use the circle punch to punch sixteen circles from the green interlining, nine circles from the yellow interlining and seven from the orange interlining. Use scissors to trim the orange and yellow circles down a little so that they are slightly smaller than the green circles.

3 Bring a needle and thread up through the edge of the interlining from the back. Thread one of the large circles, one of the smaller circles, a sequin and a bead on to the needle and slide them down to the interlining. Skip the bead and pass the needle back through the sequin and through the circles to secure the decoration to the black interlining (see detail).

4 Repeat this around the edge fourteen more times, alternating the colour of the smaller circle.

5 Decorate the crown using the remaining coloured circles, sequin and bead. Stitch it on securely.

6 Glue the crown on behind the head and allow to dry.

7 Finish by stitching a brooch back to the piece.

Queen Equinox

The colours you choose for your piece are important to define the mood.
Here, warm oranges and reds evoke an autumnal feel.

Mary, Mary, By-the-Sea

Materials:

One face charm

Small amount of medium weight iridescent bondable fibre

Metal flakes

Artgirlz 'Crown' charm

Two locks of dyed Wensleydale wool

Twenty-five gold sequins

Gold and blue seed beads

Two drilled shells

Eleven plastic fish beads

Pink, orange, green and blue peel-off marker pens

Template D, cut from non-woven black medium weight interlining

Tools:

Basic tool kit

Iron and ironing board

Instructions:

1 Make a sheet of iridescent bondable fibre by using the manufacturer's instructions, but add in some metal flakes before ironing to give extra sparkle (see detail opposite).

2 Stitch the prepared bondable fibre on to the black medium weight interlining using black thread.

3 Colour the crown with the pink and blue peel-off marker pens, then stitch it into place on top of the prepared piece.

4 Stitch the wool into position as hair.

5 Secure the face charm on top with the needle and thread to disguise the stitching, and then sew on the shell bra.

6 Embellish the lower half of the dress with sequins and beads.

7 Start the fringe by colouring the plastic fish beads with peel-off marker pens. Bring your needle and thread up through the interlining and thread on a sequin, a number of seed beads, a fish bead and a seed bead. Miss out the final seed bead and take the thread back through. Take the needle back down through the interlining to secure the embellishment to the dress.

8 Make ten more fish fringe embellishments and secure them in place.

9 Finish the piece by attaching a brooch back.

Siren Song

This compelling figure has a two-layered fringe to her dress. The shells were coloured with peel-off marker pens to give a vibrant effect.

Nefertiti

Materials:

Gold, light-coloured and dark-coloured metallic seed beads

Artgirlz charms: two 'Little Hand' and two 'Foot'

Template D cut from non-woven white heavy interlining

Two star-shaped beads

Textile glitter pen (black)

Face charm

Tools:

Basic tool kit

Instructions:

1 Colour the surface of the heavy interlining with the glitter pen. This will make any spaces between the beads less obvious.

2 Sew the face charm into position, and secure the two star-shaped beads above and below as shown.

3 Sew on the lighter-coloured metallic beads in circles around the face charm, either singly or in groups of three if you feel confident and want to work more quickly.

4 When the circle reaches the edge of the template sew the darker-coloured metallic beads in lines on to the lower half to form the robe effect, leaving the central area exposed.

5 Sew the hand and feet charms in position. Make sure the feet point in the same direction to give an ancient Egyptian look.

6 Oversew groups of three gold beads (see detail) to the edge to give a rope-like effect to the border.

7 Secure a brooch back to the piece to complete it.

Cleopatra

Turquoise, blue, lilac, black and gold were used on this piece to emphasise the opulent ancient Egyptian feel.

Miss Milly-Pede

Materials:

Template D cut from non-woven black medium weight interlining
Two 20cm (8in) square pieces of sheer nylon
Blue and pink peel-off marker pens
Purple, blue and gold seed beads
Eight assorted shoe charms
Two wooden hand charms
Artgirlz 'Mini Face' charm
Gold acrylic paint

Tools:

Basic tool kit
Medium dry felting
 needle tool
Paintbrush
Foam block

Instructions:

1 Place the first piece of sheer nylon on to the foam block and distress it with the dry felting needle tool. This creates a very particular rouched effect.

2 Rouche the second piece of nylon and place it on top of the first. Stitch them together using large running stitches in blue thread across the body (see detail opposite).

3 Cut out template D from this newly created fabric and stitch this to the black medium weight interlining templates with blue thread.

4 Position then secure the face charm with the needle and thread. Sew on gold beads around the charm, leaving large loops of beads to represent necklaces.

5 Paint the wooden hand charms with the gold paint. Once dry, take the needle up through the interlining and thread on each hand with three seed beads. Take the needle back down through the hole and secure each time.

6 Colour the shoe charms with peel-off marker pens. Thread one on to your needle along with a number of purple and blue seed beads, and attach to the body shape. Repeat with the other shoe charms.

7 To complete the piece, attach a brooch back.

Purple Janey

Is it possible to have too many shoes? The more you can fit on at the bottom of the piece, the better the effect.

Cherokee

Materials:

Template D cut from blue craft felt

Variegated pearl cotton thread

Wooden hand and feet charms

Artgirlz 'Large Face' charm

Template D cut from
non-woven black medium
weight interlining

Purple and gold acrylic paint

Fifteen blue beads

Selection of feathers

Tools:

Basic tool kit

Paintbrush

Instructions:

1 Using blanket stitch, stitch
all around the edge of the felt
template. On the head area add
beads on to the stitch to make a
'hairband' of beads.

2 Paint the hand and feet charms
with the purple and gold paint,
and add gold to the face charm.
Allow to dry.

3 Fill the body area with wheels
of blanket stitch (see detail).

4 Stitch the face, hand and feet
charms on to the body.

5 Glue the feathers into place
behind the face.

6 Stitch on the medium weight
interlining along with a brooch
back to finish.

Twinkletoes

Because feathers are so different from one another, it is easy to make a unique piece, either as a gift or just for your own pleasure.

Oh, Pearl!

Materials:

Template D cut from red craft felt

Template D cut from non-woven black medium weight interlining

Variegated pearl cotton thread

A selection of buttons

Artgirlz charms: one 'Mini Face', one 'Create Crown', two 'Glove' and two 'Little Shoe'

Gold seed beads

Ten small feature beads

Tools:

Basic tool kit

Instructions:

1 Sew blanket stitch around the edge of the craft felt with variegated cotton thread.

2 Stitch the face and crown charms into position.

3 Sew buttons all over the main body. Smaller buttons can be stitched on top of larger buttons to give a textured, layered effect.

4 Thread seed beads, feature beads and a glove charm on to a length of thread (see detail opposite) and stitch the arm into position.

5 Repeat with the other limbs, referring to the picture for how the beads are arranged on each.

6 Complete by stitching the medium weight interlining template to the piece, followed by a brooch back.

Smartiepants

These cheery colours and shapes make for a fun, eye-catching alternative.

Miss Checkmate

Materials:

20cm (8in) square of muslin

Assorted textured yarns and fibres

Artgirlz charms: one 'Heart Crown', two 'Little Hand' and two 'Striped Leg'

Face charm

A selection of seed beads, bugle beads and feature beads

Template D cut from black craft felt

Tools:

Basic tool kit

Medium dry felting needle tool

Foam block

Sewing machine

Instructions:

1 Place the muslin on top of the foam block.

2 Select a variety of yarns and fibres and place thin layers on to the muslin. Several thin layers create a better variety of texture and colour than one thick layer.

3 Needle the fibres into the background by plunging the dry felting needle tool down through and back up through the fibres. It is important to keep your needle in a vertical position as you plunge it into the mass of fibres and fabric. Gradually you will create a dry felted fabric.

4 Cut out template D from this fabric. Using variegated and solid machine threads, free machine a basic dress shape on the template, as shown opposite. When complete, cut away any excess fabric, leaving a slight edge.

5 Use the sewing machine to attach the piece to the craft felt template with black thread.

6 Sew the face and crown charms into position.

7 Thread a hand charm on to your needle along with seed beads and a feature bead, then sew the arm on to the body. Repeat with the other arm. Stitch both wrists to the body to secure.

8 Decorate the dress with the feature beads, then add strings of seed beads around the face charm. Add two feature beads as earrings on either side of the face (see detail opposite).

9 Sew the leg charms into position at the bottom.

10 Complete by sewing a brooch back on to the piece.

Lovelorn Duchess
Peel-off marker pens can be used to colour the charms for a different effect.

Wild Wanda

Materials:

20cm (8in) square of muslin

Assorted textured yarns and fibres

Gold and metallic black seed beads

Blue and pink feature beads

Template D cut from craft felt

Artgirlz charms: one 'Mini Face', five 'Little Hand' and two 'Little Shoe'

Four handbag charms

Red peel-off marker pen

Tools:

Basic tool kit

Medium dry felting needle tool

Foam block

Sewing machine

Instructions:

1 Place the muslin on top of the foam block.

2 Place several thin layers of the various yarns and fibres on to the muslin.

3 Take the needle felting tool down through and back up through the fibres repeatedly to needle the fibres into the background. Remember to keep your needle upright as you needle felt the fibres and fabric.

4 Cut out template D from this fabric and place it over the craft felt template. Using blue thread, free machine swirls and spirals to cover the background and join the two pieces.

5 Sew the face charm into position and secure a few seed and feature beads around it.

6 Create the arms by threading seed beads, feature beads and hand charms as shown in the detail opposite, then stitch them into place. Leave some free-hanging and secure the others at both the elbow and the wrist.

7 Create two legs in the same way, replacing the hands with the feet charms. Stitch on to the bottom of the body.

8 Add beads and handbag charms to embellish the remaining parts of the body.

9 Colour the charms with the red peel-off marker pen.

10 Finish by attaching a brooch back.

Venus Reclining

All dressed up with somewhere to go! Fewer handbag charms means that more of the free machine embroidery can be seen.

Tart Deco

Materials:

20cm (8in) square of muslin

Assorted textured yarns and fibres

Artgirlz charms: one 'Mini Face' and two 'Spikey Heart'

A selection of seed beads

A selection of heart-shaped and flower-shaped feature beads

Five large heart-shaped buttons in various colours

Template D cut from craft felt

Pink peel-off marker pen

Tools:

Basic tool kit

Medium dry felting needle tool

Foam block

Sewing machine

Instructions:

1 Place the muslin on top of the foam block.

2 Place several thin layers of the various yarns and fibres on to the muslin.

3 Take the dry felting needle tool up and down through the layered fibres to needle them into the background muslin. Keep your needle vertical as you work.

4 Cut out template D from this fabric, then attach it to the craft felt template with the sewing machine. Use pink thread and free machine tiny circles to cover the background (see detail opposite).

5 Sew on the face charm and stitch flower feature beads and heart buttons around it as shown.

6 Colour one of the heart charms and the face charm with the peel-off marker pen.

7 Thread the seed beads and heart feature beads on to your needle to make beaded dangles as shown, and stitch them on to the body.

8 Stitch the coloured heart charm into position.

9 Complete by mounting a brooch back to the piece.

Thirst for Romance

Various charms were added to the beaded dangles to create a bohemian effect.

San Bohemia

Instructions:

1 Attach the two pieces of medium-weight interlining together by machine stitching round the outline of the shape.

2 Stitch the face charm and arm in place, then place the flower motifs around the face and body. Sew them on securely, some with bead centres and others with decorative stitching as shown.

3 Cut out a tag-shaped piece of shrink plastic. Punch a hole in the top with the 3mm (⅛in) hole punch.

4 Use the paintbrush and the black ink pad to colour the plastic. Clean the brush and use it with the gold ink pad to paint a border around the tag.

5 Use the stamp with the gold ink pad to stamp the tag, then shrink it according to the manufacturer's instructions.

6 Use a needle and thread to attach the tag and add beads to accent the piece. Attach a brooch back to finish.

Sunbathing Flora

The flower effect on the green part of the body is achieved with solvent-based inks and a rubber stamp.

Dreamer

Materials:

Template D cut from blue-dyed mulberry (kozo) bark

Variegated cotton threads

Small amounts of lace or ribbon

Lace butterfly wing motifs

Artgirlz charms: one 'Spikey Heart', one 'Girl Face', one set of 'Wing – Butterfly' and one 'Wing – Dream'

Red, blue, orange and yellow peel-off marker pens

Clear seed beads

Three mother-of-pearl star beads

Small silver sequins

Tools:

Basic tool kit

Sewing machine

Instructions:

1 Using the variegated thread, outline the mulberry bark template with two rows of machine stitching, then free machine stitch randomly.

2 Hand sew small lazy daisy stitches over the body, securing a small silver sequin in the centre of each (see detail opposite).

3 When you have completed your stitching, sew the lace wings and butterfly wing charms to the back of the body and the face charm to the front at the top.

4 Make a trailing embellishment by threading a star bead and some seed beads on to a thread. Secure this to the body, then make two more in the same way, and one with the 'Wing – Dream' charm in place of the star bead.

5 Sew on the heart charm to cover the place where the trailing embellishments are secured, then use the peel off marker pens to colour the heart and butterfly wings.

6 Sew on a brooch back to complete the brooch.

Fly-By-Night

Dreamy purples and muted accent colours give a nocturnal feeling to this wild woman.

Acknowledgements

Tracy and Allison Stilwell, Fran Lawrence, Kathy Troup, Valdani for their threads, Magenta, Clearsnap Inc., and all those who have donated from their precious stashes.

Publisher's Note

If you would like more books on the techniques shown, try the following:
Beginner's Guide to Machine Embroidery by Pamela Watts, Search Press, 2003
The Encyclopedia of Beading Techniques by Sara Withers, Search Press, 2005
Needle Felting by Linda Lenich, Search Press, 2008